WE DIE

IN ITALY

WE DIE IN ITALY

SARAH JEAN ALEXANDER

First published by Shabby Doll House

October 2021

www.shabbydollhouse.com
@shabbydollhouse

We Die in Italy
Copyright © 2021 by Sarah Jean Alexander
All rights reserved

Front cover image by Sarah Jean Alexander
Cover design by Jake Muilenburg
Interior layout by Lucy K Shaw

Titles set in Nunito Light
Poems set in PT Serif
Cover title set in Bernoru Expanded

ISBN: 978-1-7379242-1-0

for Jake

CONTENTS

I MEAN

there was nothing groundbreaking
about my weekend
if that is what you are asking

congee
sleep
repeat

stood on a chair to reach the ceiling fan
considered our futures
in earnest

told myself
I don't have to say
anything important today

and in case you wondered —
if I'm outta here
don't worry
just come with me!

ANOTHER BEAUTIFUL SUNSET

today I sat in the sun
felt poetry come back

I suddenly and desperately craved candy
and stood in front of the pantry with a spoon
shoveling demerara sugar into my mouth

later, I will pick the wild ramps
growing across the street
I will prepare them for dinner

oh, look
another beautiful sunset

DEATH BECOMES ME

once again
I did not die
so once again
I am absolutely smothered
in indulgence
neosporin bathwater

blueberry cake
on the kitchen floor
drowned in pleasure
substituting heavy cream
for heavier cream

a thick film of butter
lining your tongue
melted onto mine
drenched yet again!

we'll split a loaf of bread for dinner
drip fat down our throats
feel strong

tomorrow I will
take a gulp of wine
too big for my mouth

let it slide down my chin
ask you
to clean me off

sometime in the future
remember me

and read this
when you care so much
that you can't care any more:

WE ARE
BAPTISED
IN SWEET
CREAM

SHAPING OUR
MOUTHS AROUND
SMALLER OCEANS

THERE IS
SO MUCH
MEDICINE
FOR OUR PAIN

EARTH TONES
AND AN
EARLY MORNING

AND LOVE
TO TAKE
WITH US
ON THE WAY

SPECTACULAR

there is a period of time
when preciousness hibernates

we go to work
and don't do anything
spectacular

there is no forward motion
of desire
at home

dead leaves creep
beneath the cracks
of window screens
and I decide to ignore them

my stomach cramps
but the world continues
to turn

there are still
potatoes to roast
bread to slice
and freeze

THE IMPORTANCE OF PICKLED HERRING

Jake says

the importance of pickled herring

to his mormor over facetime

I sit across from him

with a paper bag of pastries in my lap

skipping scones into my mouth

sucking until they dissolve

deliciously stoned

eyeing a tall glass of lemon water

the neighbor's cat at my window

who I have met before

EVEN WETTER

there have been some minor changes
in the mornings especially now
I am awake with more energy
than you might prefer

rearranging firewood before the sun
has a chance to filter through
the ceiling glass

I have never let my mood
distract from the responsibility
of being a woman and that
is a lie you accept

sometimes dill presents itself
in a way that makes eating
simply excruciating

when winter begins
it's always some kind of trick
like we want you to have fun
but you're going to suffer

a thin blanket hidden beneath
a thicker blanket
two bodies spiraling and tightly held in

I am going to be happy
regardless of how wet the earth gets
in fact I hope it gets
even wetter

if you listen closely
there is the distant sound
of someone holding hands with someone else

you can almost hear
the deep reds of their organs
pumping to fill
everything alive

DIE EROTIK

sometimes it feels
that all I have done
so far in life is work

as if it is impossible
to be indulgent

but then, I guess
there is also all of the

dancing, kissing
drugs and growing older

I simply like to be alone
and provide my own noise

I make the bed at dawn
in slow motion

all four corners of the top sheet
tucked with precision
set like a trap

KITCHEN SHIT

breakfast bowl of celery
coated in a sheen of avocado
sea salt, cccoffee

body molded
by bell peppers and lentils
fried chicken

pretend to fall asleep
to help you fall asleep
and then

eventually find some town
named after a citrus fruit
move to it

WE FEEL ANCIENT

in p.m. air we move like glaciers
massive and shrinking into each other
I am reminded of the joyful ways we feel ancient
when we love
like we have simply been

eating mustard greens and drinking melons
since the moment we first embraced
yesterday I fell asleep on the shore and woke
with a pink you feel fondness towards
blushed into the sky, tumbling home to rest and be felt

where do we go when we need to release the hum of
our human bodies and at what point do we admit
our hearts have tethered to sails?
they are somewhere across an ocean with rules
the blue, that blue green piano-looking emotion

huge like something real big, we bump wrists together
on a brisk walk like testing permissions
and it's not that I must know
that I am the most patient person alive
I just want it to be acknowledged

how long and how hard I can wait if needed
the dragonfly rests on my elbow
its neon backend flattened against sweat
stuck and relaxed
simple glow of being alive

I want to be appreciated in my steadfastness
like a perennial; purple and blooming in spring
nothing and dead in autumn
and no matter what I come back
I am the perfectly capable scorpio full moon

and have been anticipating your goneness
for like a millennium now
in the beginning I was dark and there was nothing
to see, I slowly, I became real
I loved, I loved, I became fucking evergreen

I sit down where I want
when the sun is touching my skin
we make plans for dinner
descend on asphalt
and crave

FAY

I will eat cereal tonight! brainwashed
to swallow bowls of garbage

dinner only persists because one time
a husband said it should

flipped upside down a potted plant
becomes a plant

be careful! that finger will not
regenerate

the cat will try to suffocate
herself every day

and you will compare today's tropical storm
to the warmth you feel for me

BREAD

the dough didn't have
enough time to rest and I
was too stoned to let it

this morning I thought
today would be a good day
I played some easy listening
on the radio

watched some basketball
with my husband
and the bread was disgusting

LIMONCELLO

we tuck ourselves
into bed

ankles crossed
and cool

my belly aches
like I am young again

I dream of burrata
sweet, opaque cloud

one parent dying
and then another

cliff diving and
limoncello

I dream without
saying anything

in the morning
you open the window

I roll over and over
we recross our ankles

COSMIC ROSÉ

I have
a cosmic rosé
on my tongue

to heal, drink
a glass of lambrusco
in the bathtub

my hangover cure
is light a candle at dawn

THE PERFECT ITALIAN DINNER

applying honey directly to my face as an experiment
toothpaste on a zit overnight

my husband simmers
risotto in the background

I pay my gyno bill while sitting in the dark
listening to a playlist titled *The Perfect Italian Dinner*

given that the sun had already set
I allowed the artless gesture

TERRA COTTA, OCTOBER

you thinking of me
is a phenomenon

you can feel it
wedged there
in your central nervous system
just reminding you
that hello

in Florence we are small
we are bright you are sooo
incredibly beautiful
the world is full of the both of us
it smells of terra cotta, October

frescoes and bath water
sweat and sensation
meaningless knowledge of the universe

the harvest moon
like a pit of roses

if you describe an object as milky
I am going to want to taste it

I AM LEARNING

I don't know what to say
it's just one of those
beginnings

this new emotion makes me feel like
a new day of the week
has been discovered

I watch my own hand
as it grips the carafe
methodically tilts towards another glass

it was so warm when we woke up
it felt like a mistake
something we didn't study for

we share a plate
of feta and tomatoes and barley
split an egg sunny side up

I don't know it's like
company for eternity
vows, love and etc

a room to fall asleep in
holding my face with both hands
touching your knee

with my ring finger
swapping oxygen, contemplating only
the current moment

everything else
too much too
much work

we made a home but
we can just make another
and another until we die

civilizations were only meant
to last a few hundred years
or so is what I am learning

please think of me
in passing at least
every other day

I want to be alone
with you in quiet
and feel so full

I want to be small like
a babe I want you is what
I am saying, I have to be

held I have to be
felt once
in a while

there is a silence
I am
comfortable with

I take as much of you
as I can stand
and swell

we walk towards
a literal sunset
we do not let go

ALL THE CRATERS ON VENUS ARE NAMED AFTER WOMEN

my mother cannot stop loving
in excruciating ways

my sister's ex-husband says
she is becoming more like me

two friends desperately trying
to bend it like Beckham

the less beautiful bartender
of the two bartenders
washing out the sink

Jenna Wortham eating weekday oysters
on Tompkins street

I make coffee
I clean it up

Elizabeth Bennet and
the ease of heterosexuality

I make breakfast
I clean it up

a crater on Venus
named after Mulan

my niece experiencing fascism
subconsciously on tiktok

the contemplative camgirl who sits so still
you think the video has frozen

Judith killing Holofernes
for centuries of art

a woman never pressed the *war* button
but she is capable

in general
I am very tired of thinking about children

I file my nails standing over the toilet
during a thunderstorm

I pick at the same red spot
on my chin for days

BIRDS

I don't think of you
I just feel warm like everyone else

we take big swallows from glass
and somehow nothing breaks

I make the time
for skin to skin contact

I haven't knelt in months
and cannot stop listening to birds

I recommend studying a friend's face
for as long as they can stand it

alright I am thinking about your waist
pretty often

my guy
I am absolutely vibrating

ANTAL

crying for the Hungarian novelist again
while rehydrating sourdough
inside of my mouth

I ask you to tell me something
that will make my bad dream
seem insignificant

you tell me that the stock market is crashing
and I wonder if you'd like
soup dumplings for dessert

I add a Prada dress to my cart
and stir 4 drops of stevia
into the sweet potato mash

ELAINE

trash can and smaller trash can

stretched canvas the size of a toddler

a wooden frog carrying a wooden stick

in its mouth for the percussion

curtains to hold everything in

fuchsia acrylic paint in a dot so subtle

we stare to make sure it's real

I'm a stoner now it's been proven

finally a reason to buy pretzels

and eat hummus

NAKED ANYWAY

we come home
drop our keys in the bowl
hang the hats
pet cat and inhale

refill ice cube trays
shake the makgeolli
fridge leaks but
it's alright

half a grapefruit
on the counter
and I scrub the bathtub
with sea salt and juice

funny thing
doors and walls
inside doors and walls
like we're trying to hide

in my opinion
we're always naked anyway!
tenderly slapping ass
into eternity

SOFT CHEESE

a bite of Camembert
offered to me lovingly

feels expensively warm
a full forest floor

white with stench
and a damp mouth

SOCKED IN

the temperature falls we have
drinks in the evening tiptoeing
circles around the bar

swallowing vitamins with mezcal
on vacation you touch my back
something something moves within us

ears hang low in desperation
and we trade eyes for eyes
as they move down my body

a stranger asks for money and you give it
to him, the fog rolling in already
everyone coughing towards the blur

ENNIO e TIFFANY

you make a face like

Love Theme by Ennio Morricone

I can hum it by heart and suddenly

arms floating around me, hair

one cucumber stripped and seeded

toasted sesame oil, garlic salt

I step outside like I don't need permission

there are so many rooftops

and America is connected

by one endless curb

Cinema Paradiso

begins in my lungs

I touch my knees with my elbows

I crack my toes and pounce

the radio is playing jazz again

a stranger stands too close

describing the northern lights

like Tiffany stained glass windows

pulled towards another planet

and I think I hate this but I don't

RED HOT

I go red hot inside
remembering my months in the womb

I feel embarrassed
about the possibility of god

I am so sorry
for all of our differences

and I am always dreaming
about holding limes

BREAKFAST IN PARIS

a Korean grandperson eyeballs you
no less than you eyeball them
you distractedly consider that home
has never truly existed

how do I get you happy
and keep you there
a raindrop giving up at dusk
and you are walking home to dry

a pair of twilight cockroaches
spring from the curb past your feet
city bugs longing and basically holding hands
avoiding death then daylight

I drink a tea called *Breakfast in Paris*
just to feel something
home grows smaller in consolation
some nights the moon doesn't show off at all

you can put your wrist in front of a mirror
and your wrist will reflect back
you can hold a small bouquet of flowers
and they will do the same

ARE WE

face full of
honey and cardamom
you learn that
to have a broken heart
you don't even have to love
oh you wanna give me pleasure?
hot coffee on my tongue down my
throat, I spend days thinking
about this
I want to be there
and be there
and be there
a single ten inch candlestick melts
and we wonder
are we fucking breathing wax
into our lungs
is it fucking killing us

RED WINE

am I worthy of love?
do you feel alive
when you think of me

I'm just trying to get
some damn dinner
on the table!

sorry — OK some kind of peace
just overcame me
I'm feeling calmer now

here — I made these meatballs
beef, half a can of spam
tender fat, very delicate

SO PERFECT

berries so soft they can
only be carried in mouths
ponds of color, melt and teeth

it's the next season again
and I feel forgiven

thunder follows
me everywhere

when I hold my hand out
I catch the rain and
my balance is so perfect

the forest is masculine
the sun is a hole

mushrooms as orange
as I've ever seen

I AM A GOOD PERSON

I validate others when they need validation. I don't remember everyone's name after I meet them, but I try every time. I use the almost-empty toilet paper roll before starting the new one. I think about my friends when they are not around, for no reason, for a long time. I am a good person! I wash my potatoes with a sponge and soap.

BIG SWALLOW

I cannot forget and I cannot forget
winter deepens in me
shake my hand with my hand
I'll have a ... glass of sour wine

pack my mouth with table salt
hills roll, moons set
I want nothin
for nothin in return

as tall as I'll ever be
and all parts of this body dissolving
earth opens, big swallow
just tired enough for a sweater

feed me bitch! I love you
red with contentment
mouth like an oyster
neck like lemonade

RAGE, RAGE

it is revolutionary to do something you hate
and to do it perfectly

I have started to put lemon in my water
I do 100 squats a day

the surface of the sun imprinted on your back
as you go gentle into that pussy

I AM IN CHARGE

bruised like ash, still crunchy
king of spoilt radishes

mother of marijuana
sister of mudroom
father of my brother
brother of morning person
sibling of stretching
princess of probiotics
prince of south facing window
halmoni of golden pothos
grandfather of nothing
friend of matchsticks
friend of dust
friend of doorways
friend of Brad Pitt?
friend of isolation
friend of the four of swords
friend of comfort
friend of animal teeth
friend of eucalyptus

queen of fruit flies
apple cider vinegar, rot

MMMM

weekend rom-com marathon on E!
one-hitter in the hotel bathtub
spread eagle on the mattress

sharing takeout bowls of
the world's smoothest congee

shrimp cheung fun
French wine and French wine

ok, I decide
everything needs to change, everything
become more easy

beautiful like the
Saturday through Monday
when we existed in bed

loving on and loving on
and on and on and on

I want to fuck until
the sun consumes us
lie under a blanket
sooo big that it makes you cry

hide caviar
between our teeth!
popping against
the roofs of our mmmmouths

a hand slips beneath my waistband
and I remember standing
on a balcony in Salerno ass out
as both a challenge and a gift

I set another wick on fire
and remember my resolution
to ask for help
whenever I want it

so pick up two bottles of white
on your way home tonight
pleaseee

fourteen candles surrounding the tub
blush tiles and tinned sardines
and suddenly I'm praying

to Lisbon and Saint Anthony
motherhood and tangerines
white lilies, walnut trees and forgiveness

tonight for example
just Florence:

big river small
bridges
so many women

emotional at
Piazza del Duomo
pink

Piazzale Michelangelo
sunset

I SHARE THIS WITH YOU

I don't want

to remember

not knowing you

I won't do it

not even for

a moment

you can read

too deeply

into the existence

of outer space

or you can

come here

you can

come here

it is important

that I share

this with you

the worst part

of physical pain

is it makes me

so so sad

AMOR FATI

beauty still exists
even if you can't hold it

you can stick your whole hand
into a rosebush

you can bleed
for the red of it all

and still
a flower won't save you
up closer

I'm not one to discourage
the warmth of blood
inbetween fingers

the infinite options
we have to reach it

nothing is elusive
when you really think about it

power
is in acceptance

and I feel the need
to understand
nothing

I spend half an hour
in the nursery
composing a perfect bouquet

I am in
no rush

LIFE-LIKE

I am often in pain
but I am only going to tell you now

all my friends and their
brown brown hair

I would rather be 500 years old
than happy

STEAK

hi baby
I'm always home
crack me a cold beer
pop the pine nut tips
we're freaking out drinking
a gallon of extra
pulp tangerine
cranberry lemonade
the pinks of thumbs

hi baby
the seltzer the gin
the layer of dust
top o' the fridge
fileted heirloom tomato
like the red spot of Jupiter
gravy pools great as ever
hummus so creamy
we drown

hi baby
I'm crying and I
can't get down
marshmallow pearls
leaking from
onion pores
a steak so marbled
we bury it in
the backyard

hi baby
fill me
I'm haunted by
the distortion of
a perfectly sliced
green cabbage
the veins of celery
neon and I'll say it again
fill me!

TRASTEVERE

basically,
sopping wet

tasting
calm distant wet
basil tongue

greeeen mint
cooool cocktail in
Trastevere

keeping balance
on my throat

I am thunderous
with affection
I am completely
red

I add sweet potato
to the Japanese curry

POEM ABOUT FRIENDS

I arrive at the park before the sun rises watch some highlights from last
night's baseball games on my phone shed a few tears and relax

I wish I wasn't here but then again there is nothing else for the time being
ohhhh well

at least I know where to buy an acceptable coffee, broccoli with the least
amount of larvae

at least my medium sized gold hoops, catching and releasing a cold, fall
then winter

and Willis is moving to Mexico to surf

and Meggie embraces me with and without reason

and I remember that Tori brings her own whiskey to the bar

and Evan says he knows he can successfully throw a touchdown pass in an
NFL game if given the chance

at least the quiet bench at 6 a.m. and only three turns on the bike ride to
the beach

at least I feel like an important piece amongst other important pieces and
it is a team that makes this city work

and I could walk a mile to Sam and Jordan and Brooke's with my eyes
closed

and Dom came home and then stayed here

at least we'll be together for another few months and then figure out whatever and then figure out wherever

there is always another egg to fry, clipping to pot, window to crack, temperature to feel, after the sun has set

a reason to return, uncork the Spanish white, smooth the bed sheets, etc

even without all the noise, I want it

I *prefer* to be encompassed and to take you with me

KINGDOM

garbage does not have to smell bad
it is not always full of heat, buzzing and dark

one would think it just wants
to be left alone for nearly eternity

to forget
place gratitude in time

one day become a black hole
hard reality notwithstanding

if trash could hope for possibilities
within this universe, it would

COME

there are people alive in this world
who have never looked me in the eyes
and told me what I mean to them

I don't mean to be controversial but

I discovered some new muscles
around the sides of my ass

my body is just strong enough
to feel neutral about it

if salt were a person
I would let them ruin my life

GRAZIE

thank you! to the leftover stains
from the Amalfi Coast on my sweater

to this band-aid on my wrist
where the butterknife got me real good this morning

my stomach makes big bubbles
and I give you my pain

you hold my pain
you hold it in your hands no problem

we contemplate moving our bodies
into direct sunlight

I confess to believing in the magic of hot peppers
godlike spellwork in seeds

not too unlike the pile of you
beneath the bed sheet

it's incredible
grazie

LEMON LIME MINT SALT

palms stained with dandelions
I am yellow with absolute readiness
I am so available to have
a radical time tonight thank you
first pickle back I've done in two years
and like five different routes home

we reach an agreement on the color
of mood lighting for the night
blood red on the dimmest setting
wine just comes in all shades now, orange
with skin and seed, mashed and fermented
into shared mouths, lying down, drying out,

pressing hard, black grapes and I am just
exactly aware of my longing after the sun sets
like there has never been a plan other than
sitting softly on leather, watching a corner
fill with golden hour, watermelon chilling
in lemon, lime, mint, salt

WHEN AT HOME

a small ache exists

just there
below
and behind
the perfect curve of my chin

where my body does not forget
how it never touched them
enough

don't worry

I am still
awake and on my back

dog hair from
a stranger's dog
stuck inside my clothing

a hundred bucks for a used rug
that seems too big to own
in Brooklyn

you go through two boxes
of frozen beef patties
in less than a week

we learn our new home

tomato sauce
simmering for seven hours

a bowl
straightforwardly holding
a single orange

again
this accidental rug
that almost could not unfurl

cat's litter box
housed in one
of our two closets
with winter coats and the yoga mat

I accidentally drop
the bamboo cutting board
in a fit of unnecessary
refrigerator-related frustration

replace it with a piece
of yellow plastic

monstera adansonii
enjoys the direct sunlight
less than I had
originally thought it would

baths can be
not disgusting

I learn to recognize
my face with a middle part
and you learn it
as well
unconsciously

I put all three feet
of my hair
directly on top of my head
without spillage

I learn how to recycle
according to state laws
I feel like a child

at least once a day
I make sure
that I am attentive
to stillness

and I bask in it!

currently?
all I want?

easy!

we die in Italy

quietly and together

I still go crazy
thinking about you

nothing in particular makes me feel
something else in particular

I just think us
as a whole

I don't know

something really special

And this is why, whenever I travel to Italy, I go there as if for the very last time, and why, when I first set eyes on any of its towns, it is as if I am not just returning, but bidding it farewell. Dostoevsky writes that we should live as if our every minute were the last moments of a man condemned to death: that way, we would grasp the ineffable richness of life. My impressions of Italy always feel like the last visions of a dying man.

-Antal Szerb

The Third Tower

sja

NEW YEAR'S EVE POEM

slipped
into something
a little more comfortable
short party dress house slippers
wet hair in a low bun like a founding father

face:
moisturized!
pink with makeup
and something vodka in a cup

lit all the candles
on the fireplace mantel
considered reading a book
but got very stoned instead

and now
I'm trying to think of
the last time I was in Queens
no reason, just feeling small tonight

at least
we know
which bodega sells
Strawberry Soylent
and where we can find
Lao Gan Ma in an emergency

and do you recall
when we last had oysters?
Tompkins street in the summer I just remembered

sometimes
you think nothing
is going to happen

then you smash
your face on asphalt
in Prospect Park as if you
can't handle riding a bike whilst a little drunk

u think
nothing is
happening
but then somehow
u keep remembering

anyway
at some point in the future
we may be able to get away
and see someone good while doing it

Adam Mitchell Harley
all in Hawaii and it's gonna be
really nice someday I'm sure of it

Lucy and Chris
Rachael and Kim
Mom and Pop, Jude
Mormor, Grandpa Jack
John, Shantall and Kelly
and everyone who has been
around this whole time, just farther away

Matt and Sarah
Jesse and Emma
Sloane, Spencer, Maggie
and whoever else is in fucking California right now
I can be there in six hours and I'll scream if I'm not! relax

what I really want:
shhhhhhhhhhhhhhhh
I drive us thru Tuscany
olive groves and vineyards
really really really old stone things and villas
it's obvious and absurd and yeah! it's beautiful

I'm driving us through it all again
yellow orange and green in big rolling layers

fucking ridiculous
and no one's gonna know
where we are for like, two or three weeks

just imagine
shopping for a rotisserie chicken in Paris

alright
quit your job
and I'll quit mine
I won't but I'm gonna
think about it real hard

eight candles lit
in the living room
who do I think I am
mascara on my lower lids

and it's just for me!

my gums still ache from
all of the novocaine
but hello, I can
smile now

yes I cry when I practice
but that's just what
a year does to you
sometimes

sometimes we change in permanent ways
and then sometimes we're allowed
to change just a little

I open my mouth it moves to the right
I yawn and I hurt and I am okay
my jaw cracks like a gunshot
I can feel it in my heart
and my face
goes red

I tongue my chipped
bottom front tooth
I think about gold

I tongue the other broken eight
and think about a lost treasure

sometimes the safest you can feel
is inside of a closed room
socks off standing
on a rug

sometimes you hear your neighbors' voices
and you realize there are people
holding each other
all of the time

at night I stare out my window
into everything I cannot see

with my glasses off I imagine
the streetlamp is the moon
and it is always full

it's December 31st so
you know

happy new year
I love you etc
and etc

remember to let me know where
to meet you
so soon

I'll go anywhere!

*DEATH BY CHOCOLATE
IN THE MORNING*

*I ATE SOME CAKE
BECAUSE
I WANTED TO*

*IF FEAR DID NOT EXIST
I THINK I COULD INVENT IT*

ABOUT THE AUTHOR

Sarah Jean Alexander is the author of *Wildlives*, *Loud Idiots* and *We Die in Italy*.

She wrote many of these poems in Brooklyn, New York, while wired shut with a broken jaw and drinking her meals through a straw. *We Die in Italy* was edited with her writing partner and best friend, Lucy K Shaw, in Paris and Nevers, France.

ACKNOWLEDGEMENTS

thanks to Lucy K Shaw and Jake Muilenburg.

thanks to Rachael Lee Nelson, Meggie Green, Jill Verde and Oscar d'Artois for beta reading.

thanks to group chats and the generosity of friends.

thanks to Bed-Stuy, Paris and Two Bridges.

thanks to my Vitamix and handheld vacuum.

and thanks again to Lucy, who continually helps me understand how to be alive in this world, why it's important to share how we feel, and what a friendship can be.

TROISIÈME VAGUE

by

Lucy K Shaw

Shabby Doll House, the online literary magazine (est. 2012), has published hundreds of artists and writers from all over the world.

Shabby Doll House, the publishing house (est. 2021), has published two books, and you just finished one of them. If you enjoyed it, please tell your friends. We hope to make some more soon.

For behind-the-scenes bonus content, visit:

shabbydollhouse.com/linernotes

CPSIA information can be obtained
at www.ICGtesting.com
Printed in the USA
LVHW091513221021
701199LV00012B/186

9 781737 924210